A Walk in the Bush

by Carmel Reilly

illustrated by James Cottell

OXFORD
UNIVERSITY PRESS
AUSTRALIA & NEW ZEALAND

"Do you *see* the birds?"
said Grandpa.

"I see the birds," said Mali.

"Do you see the kangaroos?"
said Grandpa.

"I see the kangaroos,"
said Mali.

"Do you see the log?"
said Mali.

"We can sit on the log," said Grandpa.

"No, Grandpa!" said Mali.
"Look at the log!"

Grandpa looked at the log.

Mali looked at the log.

"I see a snake in the log!"
said Grandpa.